i see the rhythm

paintings by michele wood
text by toyomi igus

Children's Book Press
San Francisco, CA

The Savoy Ballroom and the Cotton Club were legendary night spots in Harlem, New York City, in the 1920s through the 1940s. While everyone was welcome to try out the new dance steps at the Savoy, the Cotton Club featured entertainment for white audiences only. The Apollo Theater has been the stage for some of the most famous musicians and singers of all time—including Count Basie, Billie Holiday, and Nat "King" Cole. Although these three landmarks were actually a few blocks away from each other, artist Michele Wood has placed them side by side in her picture to create an effect of energy and excitement.

For our readers

i see the rhythm is a look at the history of African American music through the eyes of an artist.

> Michele Wood is known for her extraordinary paintings of musicians and singers. For this project, Michele read historical accounts of the early musicians and interviewed youth and elders for a community perspective. As she painted, she listened to the different styles of music and imagined herself back in the times when the music was being created. Then, I listened to the music while I looked at her paintings, and I was inspired to write poems about each musical scene. I also created a brief time line which highlights just a few of the many musical and historical events that were taking place when each style of music was being created.

i see the rhythm is a look at African American music over the past 500 years.

> There are many stories of our people in Michele Wood's paintings, and there are many more stories behind the events in the time line. Throughout our history and through all our experiences, we were always making music. Our lives influenced the music, and the music influenced our lives. In our struggle to find a place in a new land, we created music that has changed the world.
>
> We hope you enjoy our history of African American music and that you will be inspired to "see the rhythm" in your own way. We look forward to seeing your poems and stories and pictures—and to hearing the new music that you will create.
>
> You are our hope and our future, and we are waiting for your rhythms!

toyomi igus

Origins

I see the rhythm.

I see the rhythm of our beginnings.
I feel the pulse of a people and a
    land in harmony.
        I hear the legends told by the drum,
        the beats of our beliefs, the music of
            our ancient history.

Griots from the lands of Africa, pounding out
the stories of our lives—
stories of the Ibo, the Yoruba, the Bantu.

        When the slavers come,
        I feel our pulse quicken in fear.
        Our voices are silenced,
        our feet shackled,
        our dances
        stilled.

    But a new rhythm is born of our capture
    and our curse.
Our drums are now forbidden,
    but the music
            lives on in me.

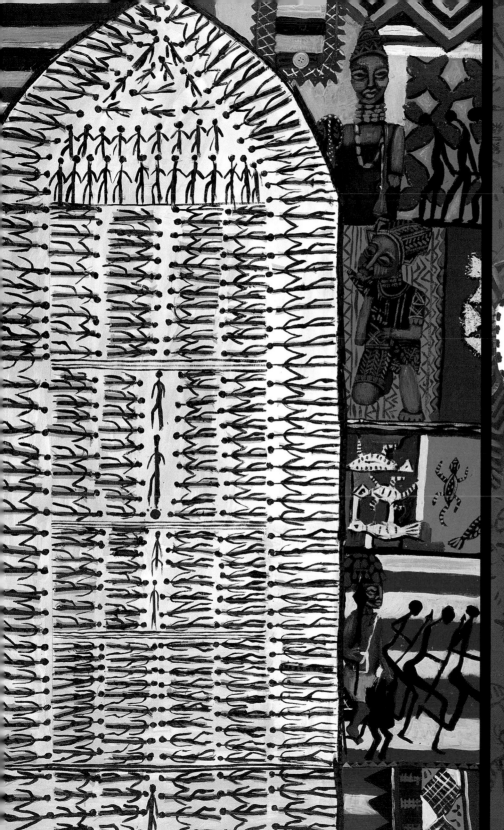

Early 1500s
European slave
traders begin buying
and capturing African
people and shipping
them across the
ocean in chains to
sell them as slaves
in the New World.
Over the next three
hundred years,
11 million Africans
survive this brutal
crossing, known as
the Middle Passage.

1619
The first boatload
of enslaved Africans
arrives in Virginia.

1630–1656
Queen Nzinga
of Angola leads
her people in the fight
against the Portuguese
slave traders.

1740s
Slave laws in the
American colonies
make it a crime for
slaves to play drums
to prevent them from
communicating with
each other in ways
their masters cannot
understand. Slaves
begin substituting
hand clapping
and foot stomps for
the drum beats.

Slave Songs

I see the rhythm of the plantation.

I hear the up swing and down swing of our labor—

swish, chop, swish, chop.
I feel the rhythms of this land—
we till, we sow, we weed, we pick—
land our fathers do not own.
I feel the rhythms of our enslaved lives—
our birth, our toil, our love, our death—
lives our mothers cannot claim.

The big bee flies high
The little bee makes the honey
The black folks make the cotton
and the white folks gets the money

These are the rhythms of slavery.

Let my people go!

Slaves sang work songs to make the hard labor easier. They also sang religious songs to give them hope that better days would come. Many of the songs had hidden messages that made fun of the slave masters or talked about the hope of freedom. Song lyrics here are from a traditional work song, "The Big Bee Flies High," and from a traditional religious song, "Let My People Go!"

1776
Congress adopts the Declaration of Independence and creates the United States of America. Although the new nation frees whites from British rule, it does not free blacks from slavery.

1831
Nat Turner leads the most famous slave revolt in U.S. history.

1849
Harriet Tubman begins helping slaves escape north to freedom on the Underground Railroad.

1850
The Fugitive Slave Act is passed, making it illegal to give shelter to runaway slaves.

1861
The Civil War begins between the North and South.

Birth of the **Blues**

I see the rhythm of the blues
in the hardship of our times—
in the calls and chants on the railroad lines.

Feelin' tomorrow like I feel today
Feelin' tomorrow like I feel today
I'll pack my bags and make my getaway.

I see the sadness of the blues
in knotted shoulder muscles
and calluses on knuckles.

I see the hope of the blues
in families dancing like there's no tomorrow
to dissolve their pain and ease their sorrow.

Everybody want to know why I sing the blues
I been down a long time, people—
I really really paid my dues.

I see the birth of the blues
in people emancipated but not yet free.

1863
President Lincoln signs the Emancipation Proclamation. Enslaved African Americans in the southern states are now free, but they are not treated equally. Many have no choice but to continue working for their former slave masters at very low pay.

1865
The Civil War ends. The 13th Amendment to the Constitution abolishes slavery in the United States.

1865–1877
Reconstruction. Blacks are promised the rights of citizens. The Freedmen's Bureau creates 4,000 schools. Over 600 black men serve in public office. Reconstruction fails when racists stop the process. Legal segregation and a separate and unequal system for blacks in the South become the law.

1871
The Fisk Jubilee Singers, an African American spiritual singing group from Fisk College, Tennessee, go on their first national tour. The funds raised save Fisk College, which was founded in 1867 to educate African Americans newly freed from slavery.

1890s
Angry mobs of white racists often attack and kill blacks and their white supporters. In response to hundreds of these brutal murders, or lynchings, African American writer and activist Ida B. Wells starts her anti-lynching campaign.

1912
The first blues song is published—"Memphis Blues" by African American composer W. C. Handy.

Ragtime is a lively
music of the late 19th
and early 20th centuries
that features the
piano and combines
European-influenced
melodies with African
American rhythms.

Ragtime

I see the rhythm of ragtime.

In our fine top hats and gowns,
we celebrate our newfound freedom
at ballroom dances and festive jubilees
where we listen to Scott Joplin's "Maple Leaf Rag"
and dare to dream of an equal world.

I see the rhythm of ragtime—
the music of the cakewalk,
the happy, high–steppin' dance of former slaves,
mimicking the high–stepping dances of their masters,
now danced by everyone.

I see the rhythm of ragtime—
in the fine, cultured places
and the optimistic faces

of free men and women.

1890s
The cakewalk becomes
a popular dance in
New York City.

1899
Scott Joplin's "Maple
Leaf Rag" becomes a
sheet-music hit, selling
75,000 copies in its
first year.

1909
The National
Association for the
Advancement of
Colored People
(NAACP) is formed in
response to the killing
of black people and the
destruction of black
businesses and homes
in Springfield, Illinois.

1910
Madame C. J. Walker
establishes a business
making pressing combs
and hair-care products
for black women. She
becomes America's first
black female
millionaire—and a
patron of black artists
and writers.

1914–1920
The Great Migration.
Thousands of black
people leave the
South for the cities
of the North to get
away from
increasing white
racist violence, to
seek work in the
steel mills and
factories, and to
provide education
for their children.

No one knows exactly when or where jazz began, but many of the early jazz musicians got their start in the Storyville section of New Orleans. In the early 1900s, jazz developed from African American folk songs, ragtime, blues, and other popular music forms.

1895
Charles "Buddy" Bolden's band is one of the first to play jazz in New Orleans.

1901
Louis "Satchmo" Armstrong is born in New Orleans. After living in poverty as a child on the streets, he learns how to play the trumpet and becomes one of the world's greatest jazz musicians.

1914–1918
World War I. Almost 400,000 black men serve in the U.S. armed forces. Even though they risk their lives for their country, they still face racism when they return home.

1917
Marcus Garvey, an immigrant from Jamaica, sets up an American chapter of the Universal Negro Improvement Association (UNIA) in Harlem, New York City. Thousands of African Americans support his back-to-Africa plan and his vision of black pride.

1923
New Orleans jazz pianist Ferdinand "Jelly Roll" Morton, one of the earliest jazz composers, makes his first recordings.

Jazz Beginnings

I see the rhythm of JaZz

in the streets of New Orleans,
where West Indian drummers catch up with
ragtime piano players and banjo-picking blues singers,

where the Dixieland sounds of marching brass bands
celebrate both fish fries and funerals,
where men who sell coal or rags by day
turn into cornet players at night and
where children, surrounded by music,
make their living singing in the streets.

I hear the slow, sad wails of funeral parade trombones
become jubilant dance music, and
from the balconies of Storyville,
I watch the birth of jazz.

12

Sounds of Swing

Swing is a jazz style played by big band orchestras from the 1920s through the 1940s. This is dance music, and people flocked to the nightclubs to stomp, boogie-woogie, and jitterbug. Song lyrics here are from "It Don't Mean a Thing (If It Ain't Got That Swing)" by Duke Ellington, 1932; and "Minnie the Moocher" by Cab Calloway, 1931.

I see the rhythm of big band jazz

in hard workin' folks steppin' out with pizzazz
to swing with the boys at the Savoy.

The finger-poppin' jazz of Fletcher Henderson,
the foot-stompin' rhythms of Louis Armstrong,
the toe-tappin' genius of Duke Ellington

make us wanna boogie-woogie all night long.

*It don't mean a thing
if it ain't got that swing.*

In the clubs uptown, the halls downtown,
I watch the world dance to the music of swing.

Hi de hi de ho.

1920S–1930S
The Harlem Renaissance. In Harlem, New York City, African American writers, artists and musicians create great works of art—and are widely recognized for their talents.

1924–1925
Louis Armstrong works with Fletcher Henderson's big band and helps develop the big band jazz sound. His incredible skill with the trumpet and his joyful personality make "Satchmo" famous all over the world.

1927
Bandleader Chick Webb leads his orchestra, the Harlem Stompers, at the famous Savoy Ballroom in New York City and becomes known as the King of the Savoy. Later, jazz singer Ella Fitzgerald joins the band.

1927–1931
Composer and bandleader Edward Kennedy "Duke" Ellington and his orchestra are booked into Harlem's famous Cotton Club. Ellington is hailed as one of this country's greatest composers.

1935
Many big swing orchestras disband for lack of work due to the Great Depression.

A Tribute to the JazzWomen

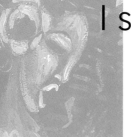

I see the rhythm of the jazz women

and in their voices I hear the blues influences of

Ma Rainey

and Bessie Smith.

I hear their voices echo the instruments of jazz,
sounding like the sax and the trumpet.

I smile with Ella Fitzgerald as she sings, scats and
becomes the First Lady of Song.

I sigh with Sarah Vaughan as she stretches the lyrics
and becomes the Divine Sarah.

I cry with Billie Holiday as she struggles through life
and becomes Lady Day, the voice of black women in America.

Mama may have, Papa may have,
But God bless the child that's got his own ...
That's got his own ...

In the many beautiful voices of our jazz women,
I see the essence of jazz.

1920
Singer Mamie Smith's recording of "Crazy Blues" becomes a surprise hit. White record companies begin making records by and for black people. The new records are called "race records."

1923
Bessie Smith, known as the Empress of the Blues, signs a contract with Columbia and becomes black music's first recording superstar.

1934
Ella Fitzgerald joins Chick Webb's band at age 17.

1939
Billie Holiday records "Strange Fruit," a song about lynching. The recording makes her nationally famous.

Opera singer Marian Anderson is barred from singing in Constitution Hall in Washington, D. C., because she is black. Instead, she sings to a crowd of 75,000 from the steps of the Lincoln Memorial.

Bertha Hill
Ethel Waters
Billie Holiday
Sarah Vaughan
Abbey Lincoln
Sylvia Syms
Evelyn White

Michele Wo

BeBop

Bebop is a jazz style created during the early 1940s. It was played by small groups and featured fast tempos, complex harmonies, and highly creative improvisations. Unlike swing, bebop is a music for listening rather than for dancing.

I see the rhythm of bebop,

the music of those jazz hipsters

who refuse to play the dance rhythms of swing
and experiment with sound at Minton's Playhouse in
Harlem and the clubs of 52nd Street.

There, we dig the flights of fancy from Charlie Parker's sax,

the inventive harmonies of Thelonious Monk's piano,

and the Latin rhythms of Chano Pozo's congas.

There, in our zoot suits,  porkpie hats and shades we are the living end.

I see the rhythm
in the new sound,
the new style,
the new attitude—

bebop.

1939–1945
World War II. Over 1 million black men serve in "colored" units in the segregated armed services. For many, their lives are changed by the respect they receive in Europe. They return home demanding more rights. Many black musicians make Europe their home.

1940s
Minton's Playhouse, a Harlem, New York City, nightclub, becomes the early home of bebop. Pianist Thelonious Monk plays in the house band and saxophonist Charlie "Bird" Parker sits in. Later, the downtown clubs of 52nd Street become the centers of the bebop movement.

1947
Trumpeter Dizzy Gillespie records "Cubana Be" and "Cubana Bop," combining jazz with conga drummer Chano Pozo's Cuban rhythms. The Afro-Cuban influence in jazz begins.

1948
Under pressure from black groups, President Harry Truman desegregates the armed forces.

1956
Dizzy Gillespie is sent around the world by the U.S. State Department as the Ambassador of Jazz.

Under the influence of
trumpeter Miles Davis,
cool jazz developed in
the late 1940s and
1950s. It features a
cool, sparse, laid-back
sound—very different
from bebop, which is
fast and intense.

cool JazZ

I see the rhythm of cool jazz in the music of young musicians

crying out for freedom of expression.

1949
Miles Davis releases
the *Birth of the Cool*
album with white
arranger Gil Evans. Cool
jazz becomes popular
among young, "cool"
college students.

1954
Drummer Max Roach,
who played with all of
the great bebop
musicians in the 1940s,
forms his own band,
the Max Roach/Clifford
Brown Quintet.

In the case of *Brown v.
Board of Education*, the
United States Supreme
Court rules that
segregation in public
education is
unconstitutional.

1955
Saxophonist John
Coltrane joins the Miles
Davis Quintet.

1957
Nine black teenagers
attempt to integrate the
all-white Central High
School in Little Rock,
Arkansas. Governor Orval
Faubus calls in the
National Guard to prevent
them from enrolling.
In response, composer
and jazz bassist Charles
Mingus writes "Fables
of Faubus."

I hear the smooth sounds of Miles' trumpet,

the hard bop beats of Roach's drums,

the cosmic waves of Coltrane's sax

in the sounds of

subway trains racing through tunnels
hard-heeled footsteps on concrete sidewalks
flashing lights atop tall steel towers.

Cool jazz—a music of city tempos
made by people locked into city rhythms.

From the basements to the rooftops,
I see the cool tones of modern jazz
escape the city heat.

The Spirit of Gospel

Gospel, the sacred religious music of African American Christians, has its roots in the religious folk songs or spirituals of slavery times. In the 1930s, performers and composers began writing a new style of religious music that became known as gospel. Song lyrics here are from the traditional spiritual, "He's Got the Whole World in His Hands."

1932
Sallie Martin and Reverend Thomas Andrew Dorsey, the Father of Gospel Music, organize the National Convention of Gospel Choirs and Choruses and create the gospel music concert circuit.

1947
Gospel singer Mahalia Jackson records "Move On Up a Little Higher" which sells a million copies, and she becomes internationally famous.

1954
Aretha Franklin, at age 12, starts singing in her father's church choir. Later, she is known as the Queen of Soul.

1955
Activist Rosa Parks is arrested in Montgomery, Alabama, when she refuses to give her seat on a bus to a white man. This action triggers a year-long successful black boycott of buses in Montgomery.

1960
Activist Septima Clarke travels all over the South setting up citizenship schools to help poor rural blacks pass literacy tests so they can register to vote.

I see the rhythm of gospel—
the music that makes us rock in the pews, testifying.
I hear the deep mellow voices of our grandparents
who nod in remembrance as they sing,

the firm resolved voices of our parents
who draw strength for the struggle from the music,

the bright young voices of our children,
who are eager to claim their place in the world.

He's got you and me brother,
in His hands.
He's got you and me sister,
in His hands.

In church on Sunday morning,
I see the rhythm of gospel
and the heart of rhythm and blues.

Amen.

Rhythm & Blues / Soul Music

1953
VeeJay Records joins Chess Records and others on Chicago's Record Row. All over the country, independent recording companies are discovering and promoting new black R&B and jazz talents. Many of these companies are black owned.

1960
Stax Records ("Soulsville USA") is founded in Memphis, Tennessee.

Black students protest racial segregation by sitting in at white-only lunch counters in the South.

1961
Barry Gordy forms Motown Records ("Hitsville USA") in Detroit, Michigan.

1963
Over 200,000 people demonstrate at the March on Washington for Jobs and Freedom. Dr. Martin Luther King, Jr., delivers his famous "I Have a Dream" speech.

1964
President Lyndon Baines Johnson signs the historic Civil Rights Act of 1964, outlawing discrimination in housing, employment, and education.

1965
Black leader and activist Malcom X is assassinated.

1967
Aretha Franklin's "Respect" hits the top of the charts.

Rhythm and blues (R&B) evolved from blues, jazz, and gospel. In the 1960s, it became known as soul music. It combines blues-style lyrics about everyday life with the gospel style of singing. Song lyrics here are from "Say It Loud—I'm Black and I'm Proud" by James Brown, 1968. Brown is known as the Godfather of Soul.

I see the rhythm of soul music,
resonate from our record players
and radiate from our radios.
WVON—the voice of the Negro—
brings us news of race riots
and hits from Hitsville USA.
Out there we struggle for an equal chance,

but inside our homes we dance, dance, dance
to recordings from
Chess Records, Curtom, VeeJay and Stax.
The Motown Revue sends buses of soul singers
to fill our inner-city stages with music.

There I see the rhythm of soul,
in familiar voices that now sing a new message:

Say it loud—
I'm black
and I'm proud.

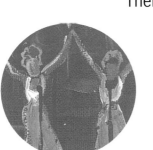

black Rock

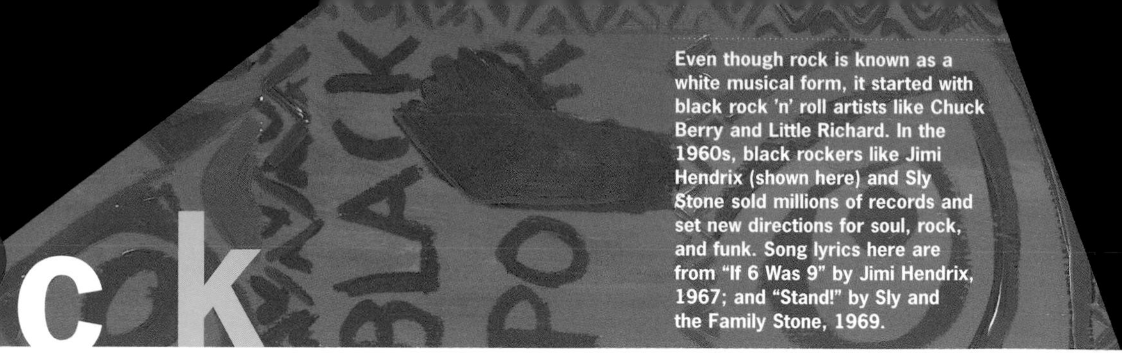

Even though rock is known as a white musical form, it started with black rock 'n' roll artists like Chuck Berry and Little Richard. In the 1960s, black rockers like Jimi Hendrix (shown here) and Sly Stone sold millions of records and set new directions for soul, rock, and funk. Song lyrics here are from "If 6 Was 9" by Jimi Hendrix, 1967; and "Stand!" by Sly and the Family Stone, 1969.

1955
Chuck Berry records his first big hit, "Maybelline," for Chess Records. Berry's style of electric guitar playing helps make the electric guitar the main instrument of rock 'n' roll.

1955–1959
Little Richard makes a string of rock 'n' roll recordings, including "Tutti Frutti" (1956) and "Good Golly, Miss Molly" (1958). He becomes known as the King of Rock 'n' Roll.

1966
Huey Newton and Bobby Seale form the Black Panther party in Oakland, California. Free breakfast programs for children and free clinics in black communities are part of their militant program for community control of schools, police, and other public agencies.

1968
Dr. Martin Luther King, Jr., is assassinated. Race riots erupt in 125 cities. Black athletes at the Olympic Games in Mexico City give the black power salute in support of civil rights and in protest of the Vietnam War.

1969
The U.S. puts the first man on the moon.

Jimi Hendrix and Sly and the Family Stone play at the Woodstock Festival, the largest outdoor rock concert ever held. Jimi Hendrix plays an explosive guitar solo of "The Star-Spangled Banner."

I see the rhythm of rock 'n' roll
in the urban riots and student protests of the sixties.
I watch the live wires of rock 'n' roll explode under pressure—
the heavy metal riffs of Jimi Hendrix

They're hoping soon my kind will drop and die

but I'm gonna wave my freak flag high, high ...

and the psychedelic grooves of Sly Stone.

STAND! *In the end you'll still be you ...*

The music expresses the rage and people plug into the power.
Black, white, Asian, Latino voices chant together
for civil rights and world peace.

I see the rhythm of rock 'n' roll
in the energy of the age of Aquarius.

26

FUnK

The funk sound is characterized by strong syncopated rhythms. In the 1970s, the heavy bass beats of funk can also be found in disco, jazz, and rock. But it was the African-based philosophy, the wild, colorful costumes, and the dance grooves of the group Parliament-Funkadelics, that became best known as funk. Song lyrics here are from "One Nation Under a Groove" by Parliament-Funkadelics, 1978.

I see the rhythm of FUnK
in the clubs, where the music of
Earth, Wind and Fire
and Kool and the Gang
bring us to our feet.
In the concert halls, we watch
as the Mothership lands
to the driving beat

of P-Funk and Bootsy's Rubber Band.

With our Afro'd minds and sequined souls,
we have come to Earth to move the music
to a new level.

*One nation
under a groove*
nothing can stop us now.

1967
James Brown leads the way into funk with his hit record, "Cold Sweat."

1968
After two years of struggle by black students, San Francisco State College (SFSC) establishes the first Black Studies Department, which also offers the first bachelor's degree in Black Studies. SFSC's efforts are quickly copied by other university campuses around the country.

1972
The United States ends its war with Vietnam.

1975
Earth, Wind and Fire's fusion of funk/jazz/latin/soul styles becomes wildly popular. Audiences of all cultures and countries buy their album, *That's the Way of the World.*

1976
George Clinton and his group Parliament-Funkadelics (or P-Funk) release their pioneering album, *The Mothership Connection.* The following year, P-Funk's Mothership Connection Earth Tour show includes landing a "spaceship" right on stage.

rap/**hip** hop

In the 1970s and 1980s, young musicians and deejays start creating a new music in the streets—hip hop. Rapping (rhyming in rhythm over the beats), scratching (where a turntable needle is rubbed over a record to create a scratching sound), and sampling (where pieces of prerecorded music are put together to create a new music) are what make hip hop music distinctive. Lyrics here are from "The Message" by Grandmaster Flash and the Furious Five, 1982; and "Africa's Inside Me" by Arrested Development, 1994.

I see the rhythm of h i p h o p

dig its way out with a shout
from the urban underground
of boomboxes and block parties
to hit the top of the charts.

Don't–push–me–cause–I'm–close–to–the–edge!

I see young rappers
seek answers, speak truths,
and reconnect
to the Motherland.

Africa's inside me
taking back her child.
She's giving me my pride
and setting me free ...

Fathered by funk and nurtured by mother Africa,

I see the rhythm of h i p h o p
and the rhythm lives on in me.

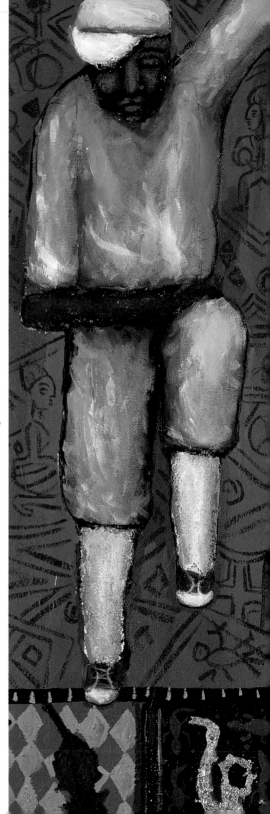

Early 1970s

Groups of black and Latino youth in the South Bronx, New York City, launch the hip hop movement, which incorporates rap music, graffiti art, and break dancing.

1979

Grandmaster Flash and his group, the Furious Five, known for their messages of social criticism, cut the first authentic Bronx rap record, "Super Rappin."

A New Jersey–based group, the Sugar Hill Gang, records "Rapper's Delight," which sells 10 million copies worldwide.

1983

Russell Simmons founds Def Jam Records, which becomes the world's best known rap label, recording LL Cool J, Public Enemy, Jazzy Jeff, and the Fresh Prince.

Jessie Jackson declares his candidacy for president of the United States.

1989

Queen Latifah's "Mama Gave Birth to the Soul Children" expresses hip hop pride in African culture and history.

1990s

Popular hip hop groups incorporate music from Africa and the African Diaspora in order to create new sounds.

i see the rhythm

Michele Wood is a painter, media artist, and printmaker whose work has gained wide recognition in the United States, Canada, and Nigeria. Her first book, *Going Back Home*, received the 1997 American Book Award and was highly praised for its stunning art and powerful, personal treatment of African American history. She lives in Atlanta, Georgia.

Toyomi Igus is the author and editor of several books for children, including *Two Mrs. Gibsons* and the award-winning *Going Back Home*, her brilliant account of artist Michele Wood's personal journey to the South. The former Editor and Publications Director for UCLA's Center for African American Studies, she lives in Los Angeles, California.

To God Almighty and to the next generation of artists—
the greater the vision, the more we see what is yet to be achieved.
You must live your song.

–M.W.

For my children and all children—especially one young Oakland lady,
who sings and sees the rhythm very clearly.

–T.I.

looking for missy

Artist Michele Wood put a little girl named Missy in every scene. Missy was Michele's nickname when she was growing up. Sometimes it's easy to find her, but sometimes it isn't. In the first scene, Missy is a little baby on her mother's back. In the swing scene, she's hiding in the bass watching the dancers. Later, with the jazz women, she's playing her own piano. Maybe she will be a great musician too, one day. And in the last scene, that's her in the middle, just graduated from college and looking forward to the future. See if you can find her in the other scenes.

Editor: Harriet Rohmer
Consulting Editors: Bil Banks, Professor of African American Studies, University of California at Berkeley, and David Schecter
Design and Production: Tenazas Design
Editorial/Production Assistant: Laura Atkins

Thanks to the staff of Children's Book Press: Sharon Bliss, Shannon Keating, Janet Levin, Emily Romero, Stephanie Sloan, and Christina Tarango.

Children's Book Press is a nonprofit publisher of multicultural literature for children, supported in part by grants from the California Arts Council.
Write us for a complimentary catalog:
Children's Book Press, 246 First Street, Suite 101, San Francisco, CA 94105

Distributed to the book trade by Publishers Group West.

Library of Congress Cataloging-in-Publication Data
Igus, Toyomi
I See the Rhythm / text by Toyomi Igus ; paintings by Michele Wood.   p.   cm.
Summary: Chronicles and captures poetically the history, mood, and movement of African American music.
ISBN 0-89239-151-0 (hardcover)
1. Afro-Americans—Music—History and criticism—Juvenile literature.
[1. Afro-Americans—Music—History and criticism.]
I. Wood, Michele, ill. II. Title.
ML3556.I48   1998   780'.89'96073—DC21   97-29310   CIP   MN   AC

Printed in Singapore by Tien Wah Press, Ltd.
10   9   8   7   6   5   4   3   2